WEST CHICAGO PUBLIC LIBRARY DISTRICT

3 6653 00120 0322

12/02

P9-CML-122

taped pgs

West Chicago Public Library District
118 West Washington
West Chicago, IL 60185-2803
Phone # (630) 231-1552

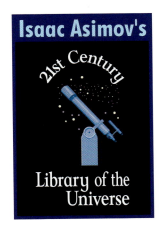

Isaac Asimov's

21st Century

Library of the
Universe

The Solar System

Asteroids

BY ISAAC ASIMOV

WITH REVISIONS AND UPDATING BY RICHARD HANTULA

Gareth Stevens Publishing

A WORLD ALMANAC EDUCATION GROUP COMPANY

Please visit our web site at: www.garethstevens.com
For a free color catalog describing Gareth Stevens Publishing's list of high-quality
books and multimedia programs, call 1-800-542-2595 (USA) or 1-800-387-3178 (Canada).
Gareth Stevens Publishing's fax: (414) 332-3567.

The reproduction rights to all photographs and illustrations in this book are controlled by the individuals
or institutions credited on page 32 and may not be reproduced without their permission.

Library of Congress Cataloging-in-Publication Data

Asimov, Isaac.
   Asteroids / by Isaac Asimov; with revisions and updating by Richard Hantula.
      p. cm. — (Isaac Asimov's 21st century library of the universe. The solar system)
   Rev. ed. of: Cosmic debris: the asteroids. 1994.
   Summary: Introduces the bodies in space also known as planetoids, minor planets,
or when they stray from their paths, meteoroids.
   Includes bibliographical references and index.
   ISBN 0-8368-3233-7 (lib. bdg.)
   1. Asteroids—Juvenile literature. [1. Asteroids.] I. Hantula, Richard. II. Asimov,
Isaac. Cosmic debris: the asteroids. III. Title. IV. Isaac Asimov's 21st century library
of the universe. Solar system.
QB651.A84   2002
523.44—dc21
                                                  2002021685

This edition first published in 2002 by
Gareth Stevens Publishing
A World Almanac Education Group Company
330 West Olive Street, Suite 100
Milwaukee, WI 53212 USA

Revised and updated edition © 2002 by Gareth Stevens, Inc. Original edition published in 1988
by Gareth Stevens, Inc. under the title *The Asteroids*. Second edition published in 1994 by
Gareth Stevens, Inc. under the title *Cosmic Debris: The Asteroids*. Text © 2002 by Nightfall, Inc.
End matter and revisions © 2002 by Gareth Stevens, Inc.

Series editor: Betsy Rasmussen
Cover design and layout adaptation: Melissa Valuch
Picture research: Kathy Keller
Additional picture research: Diane Laska-Swanke
Artwork commissioning: Kathy Keller and Laurie Shock
Production director: Susan Ashley

The editors at Gareth Stevens Publishing have selected science author Richard Hantula to bring
this classic series of young people's information books up to date. Richard Hantula has written
and edited books and articles on science and technology for more than two decades. He was
the senior U.S. editor for the *Macmillan Encyclopedia of Science*.

In addition to Hantula's contribution to this most recent edition, the editors would like to
acknowledge the participation of two noted science authors, Greg Walz-Chojnacki and
Francis Reddy, as contributors to earlier editions of this work.

All rights to this edition reserved to Gareth Stevens, Inc. No part of this book may be reproduced,
stored in a retrieval system, or transmitted in any form or by any means, electronic, mechanical,
photocopying, recording, or otherwise, without the prior written permission of the publisher except
for the inclusion of brief quotations in an acknowledged review.

Printed in the United States of America

1 2 3 4 5 6 7 8 9 06 05 04 03 02

Contents

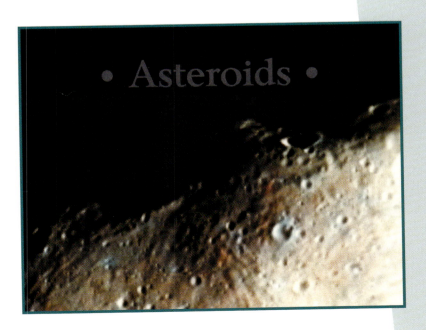

We live in an enormously large place – the Universe. It is only natural that we would want to understand this place, so scientists and engineers have developed instruments and spacecrafts that have told us far more about the Universe than we could possibly imagine.

We have seen planets up close, and spacecrafts have even landed on some. We have learned about quasars and pulsars, super-novas and colliding galaxies, and black holes and dark matter. We have gathered amazing data about how the Universe may have come into being and how it may end. Nothing could be more astonishing.

Many of the objects in the Universe are huge, but many small objects exist in space, as well. These objects would be too small to see if they were very far away from Earth, but some of them are right here in our own Solar System. Hundreds of thousands of minor planets called asteroids travel around the Sun in orbits just as planets do. Some come very close to us, some stay quite far away, and some follow peculiar orbits. Asteroids come in a variety of shapes and sizes.

To Be or Not to Be — A Planet?

When is a planet not a planet? When it is an asteroid.

Ceres is a body in space that was discovered in 1801 between the orbits of Mars and Jupiter. It is smaller than any planet — only about 590 miles (950 kilometers) across. Astronomers later found still more objects in the same region, all of them even smaller than Ceres. Astronomers called them minor planets or planetoids. They also referred to the bodies as *asteroids*, which means "starlike." When astronomers looked through their telescopes, asteroids — because they are so tiny — seemed to be dots of light that resembled stars.

Astronomers are constantly on the lookout for new asteroids. By the year 2001, they had found more than 150,000 of these minor planets and had already figured out the orbits of more than 30,000 of them.

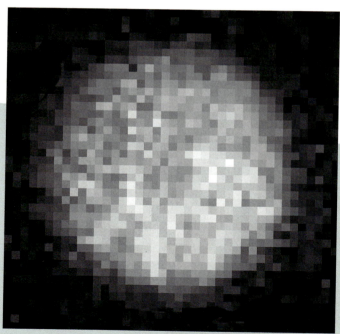

Above: Ceres, as seen by the Hubble Space Telescope.

An artist's conception of the asteroids, as viewed from just beyond Jupiter. Also clearly visible are Mars, which is within the belt of asteroids, and Earth. Near the Sun, which glows faintly from about 500 million miles (800 million km) away, Venus and Mercury are visible.

The Missing Planet?

Even before Ceres was found, astronomers were looking for these asteroids, even though they may not have realized it. One astronomer had noticed that most planets in the Solar System seemed to be spaced in a regular pattern. The space between Mars and Jupiter did not fit the pattern, however. The large space between these planets led astronomers to believe there might be another planet in between them. The planet would have to be a small one or else it would already have been discovered. When Ceres was found, astronomers thought it was the missing planet. The real surprise came when they found not one, but thousands of little planets in the space between Mars and Jupiter! This space is called the asteroid belt.

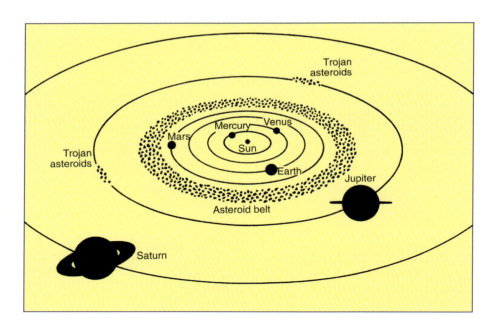

Stumbling onto Ceres

Almost 200 years ago, a group of German astronomers planned to search the heavens for a possible planet between Mars and Jupiter. They carefully divided sections of the sky among themselves. Just before they were ready to start, word came that Italian astronomer Giuseppe Piazzi, who was not looking for a new planet at all, happened to stumble onto Ceres while he was watching for other objects. He discovered Ceres on January 1, 1801. He named the new object after the ancient Roman goddess of agriculture.

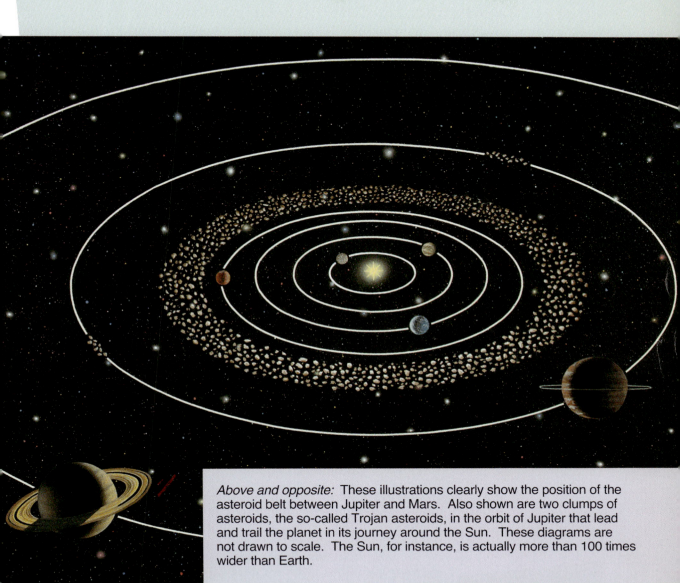

Above and opposite: These illustrations clearly show the position of the asteroid belt between Jupiter and Mars. Also shown are two clumps of asteroids, the so-called Trojan asteroids, in the orbit of Jupiter that lead and trail the planet in its journey around the Sun. These diagrams are not drawn to scale. The Sun, for instance, is actually more than 100 times wider than Earth.

The Many Sizes and Shapes of Asteroids

No asteroid bigger than Ceres has ever been found in the asteroid belt, but dozens that are more than 100 miles (160 km) across do exist. Most asteroids, however, are less than a mile across. Only the largest asteroids look round. Small asteroids have different shapes. The asteroid called Kleopatra, for example, looks like a dog bone.

Some of the larger asteroids have been found to have tiny moons. Dactyl, the moon of the asteroid Ida, is only about one mile (1.6 km) across. Many asteroids are dark, but some are bright. One of the earliest asteroids discovered was Vesta. It reflects so much light that sometimes it can be faintly seen without a telescope.

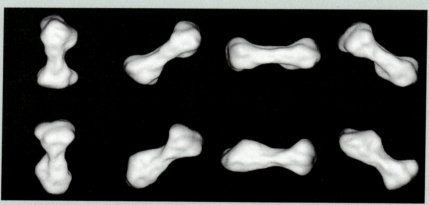

Above: Several images of the dog-bone-shaped asteroid Kleopatra.

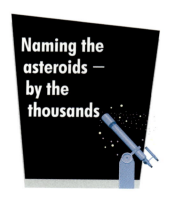

Naming the asteroids — by the thousands

At first, asteroids were named after goddesses, such as Ceres, Pallas, Vesta, Juno, and so on. When great numbers of asteroids were discovered, however, it became difficult to name them all. They began to be named for astronomers, famous people, friends, cities, colleges, and so on. From the beginning, most of the names were feminine, such as Washingtonia and Rockefellia. The first asteroid to get a masculine name was Eros, who was the ancient Greek god of love, in 1898. One asteroid originally was named Drake, but to make the name different, perhaps more feminine, it was spelled backwards as Ekard.

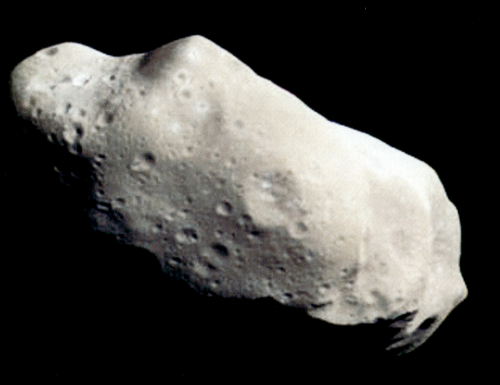

This color shot of the asteroid Ida and its moon Dactyl was made from images taken by the imaging system on the *Galileo* spacecraft on August 28, 1993.

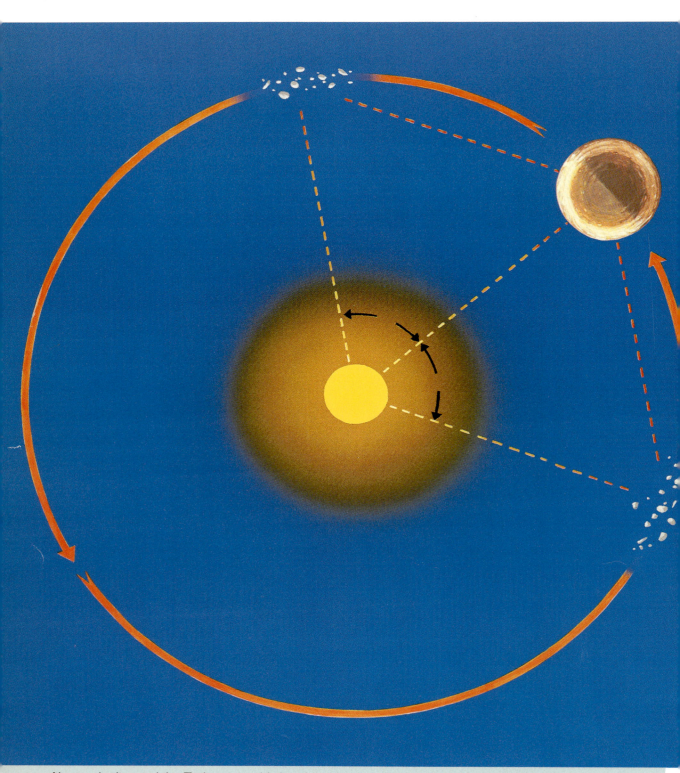

Above: Jupiter and the Trojan asteroids in orbit. In their trek around the Sun, Jupiter and its army of asteroids hold to a steady formation.

Jupiter's Captured Moons

Jupiter, the huge planet at the outer edge of the asteroid belt, has captured many asteroids. It has more than two dozen moons circling it, and some of them are probably asteroids that it has trapped. Also connected with Jupiter are the asteroids known as *Trojans*. Some of these asteroids follow Jupiter in its orbit, and others move ahead of it in its orbit. If you draw a line from Jupiter to each of these two groups of asteroids, and then draw lines from Jupiter and both groups to the Sun, you will have two equal-sided triangles. The asteroids are named Trojans in honor of heroes in ancient Greek tales about the Trojan War.

Above: A close-up view of one of Jupiter's Trojan asteroids called Hector. Is Hector a single dumbbell-shaped asteroid or two asteroids stuck together?

Above: The asteroid Hidalgo *(right)* seems to dwarf Jupiter as it approaches the planet in the far reaches of our Solar System beyond the asteroid belt.

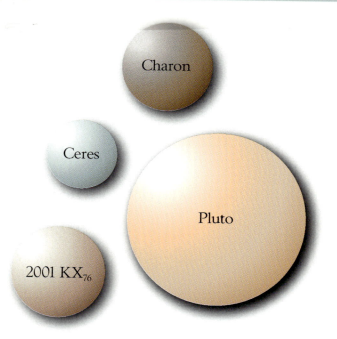

Left: This drawing shows a comparison of the sizes of Pluto, Charon, Ceres, and 2001 KX$_{76}$.

Beyond the Asteroid Belt

Some asteroids lie far beyond the asteroid belt — beyond even Jupiter and its faithful family of asteroids. The asteroid Hidalgo has a long orbit that takes it from the asteroid belt to a point just past the orbit of Saturn. A group of small bodies called Centaurs travel around the Sun in the space between the orbits of Jupiter and Neptune. Another group of objects, whose orbits lie beyond Neptune, make up the Kuiper Belt, which is named after the astronomer Gerard Kuiper. Most of the Centaurs and Kuiper Belt objects are icy comets. Some, however, may be rocky asteroids. In 2001, astronomers found an object in the Kuiper Belt that may be larger than Ceres. It was called 2001 KX_{76}.

Some of the moons of the planets beyond Jupiter may be captured asteroids. Some astronomers even think that the farthest known planet, Pluto, and its moon Charon should be considered asteroids, because they are so small.

Sizing up Ceres — big asteroid or little planet?

When Ceres was discovered, everyone was surprised at how small it was. It is only about 590 miles (950 km) across, about the width of France; while Mercury, the smallest planet then known, is over 3,000 miles (4,800 km) across, about the width of North America. As more and more asteroids were discovered, however, astronomers were surprised at how big Ceres was in comparison. Its diameter was twice as large as the diameter of the second-biggest asteroid in the asteroid belt. In fact, some astronomers calculate that Ceres has $1/3$ as much mass as all the asteroids in the asteroid belt put together. Why is it so large? Scientists do not know.

Asteroids or Comets?

We know that many asteroids are found between Mars and Jupiter, while others lie even farther out. Not all asteroids behave in the same way, however. A few have long, thin orbits that take them much closer to the Sun than others. Such orbits resemble those of some comet orbits. Astronomers have carefully studied the light from some of these asteroids and have found that in some cases the light looks much like the light from comets. It is possible that some asteroids traveling near the Sun may actually be old comets that have lost their ice and no longer glow like ordinary comets.

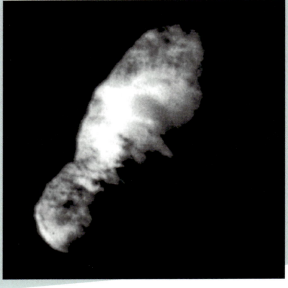

Right: A NASA picture of the comet Borrelly.

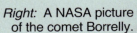

A different sort of asteroid — but why?

The brightest asteroid is Vesta. It is the third-largest asteroid at 326 miles (525 km) across, but it is only about $1/2$ the size of Ceres. Vesta reflects much more light than Ceres, however. In fact, if you know exactly where to look and have very sharp eyes, you can see Vesta without a telescope. Yet it was only the fourth asteroid to be found. By studying the light from Vesta, scientists have learned that at one time much of the surface of Vesta was melted. Perhaps it was covered with lava. Most other asteroids seem to have always been cold rock. Why should Vesta be so different? Scientists are not sure.

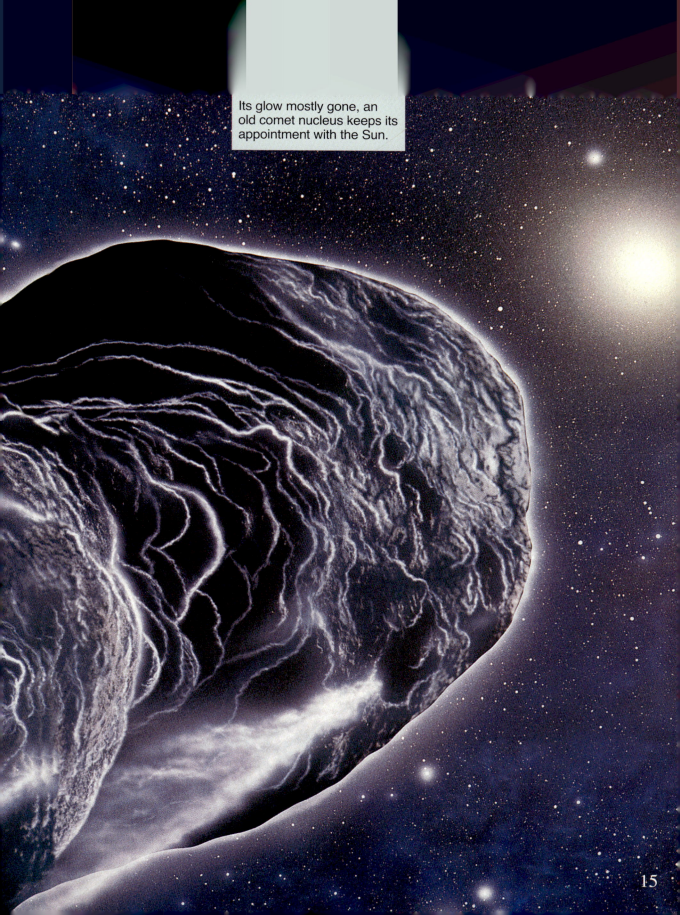

Its glow mostly gone, an old comet nucleus keeps its appointment with the Sun.

Above: A remarkable event in 1972 captured in a photo. Having entered Earth's atmosphere over Idaho, an asteroid — now a streaking meteor — flies above Jackson Lake, Wyoming. Astronomers believe it was 260 feet (80 m) in diameter, moved at an average speed of 33,000 miles (53,000 km) per hour, and weighed 1,000,000 tons.

Right: A photo of the Leonid meteor shower streaking through Earth's atmosphere. The Leonid shower occurs every year, but it tends to be exceptionally heavy every 33 years. The latest heavy shower was in 1999, so the next one should occur in 2032.

A Threat to Earth?

For a long time, astronomers thought of asteroids as members of the outer Solar System, beyond Mars. In 1932, though, an asteroid named Amor was discovered. This object had an orbit that took it between the asteroid belt and Earth. In 1937, a small asteroid named Hermes passed within 488,000 miles (785,000 km) of Earth. Scientists came to realize that asteroids — and comets, which also contain rock — were a possible threat to our planet.

Collisions have occurred in the past. In Arizona, there is a crater 3/4 mile (1.2 km) across where an asteroid struck 50,000 years ago. Asteroids and comets that travel close to Earth's orbit are called near-Earth objects. Hundreds of such objects have been discovered that are at least 3/5 mile (1 km) wide. None of the known objects of this size is likely to collide with Earth. Smaller bodies, however, occasionally do strike Earth or explode in Earth's atmosphere. Usually these are tiny objects and no great harm is done, but a small asteroid that exploded in the air over Siberia, in Russia, in 1908 knocked down tens of thousands of trees.

An artist's conception of a killer asteroid striking Earth.

Picture Perfect

Our first hints of what asteroids might look like came in the 1970s when the *Viking* probes got a good view of the moons of Mars — Phobos and Deimos. These moons are dark, lumpy objects that fit the idea astronomers had of asteroids.

In the 1990s, the spacecraft *Galileo* looped through the asteroid belt twice on its way toward Jupiter. It snapped our first clear pictures of true asteroids — Gaspra and Ida.

The probe *Deep Space 1* took a close look at the near-Earth asteroid called Braille in 1999. The probe *NEAR-Shoemaker* (*NEAR* in the probe's name stood for "Near Earth Asteroid Rendezvous") took close-up pictures of the near-Earth asteroid Mathilde in 1997, and then flew on to study another near-Earth asteroid, Eros. In 2001, the probe landed on Eros — the first landing ever made by a spacecraft on an asteroid.

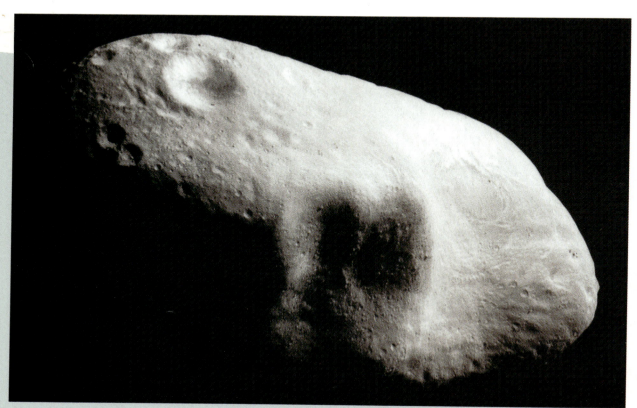

Above: An image of Eros, taken by the spacecraft *NEAR-Shoemaker*'s multispectral imager on March 3, 2000.

This composite picture shows two moons and an asteroid — but they look similar to one another. The upper object is the asteroid Gaspra, which lies between Mars and Jupiter and belongs to the Flora family of asteroids. Gaspra's picture was taken by the *Galileo* probe in 1991. The two lower objects are Phobos *(left)* and Deimos *(right)*, the moons of Mars. Their pictures were taken by the *Viking* spacecraft in 1976. Astronomers suspect that Mars's moons are really asteroids that wandered too close to Mars and were captured by the planet's gravity.

Space Mining

Asteroids that are just a few feet across are called meteoroids. We see them as meteors when they enter Earth's atmosphere. If they strike Earth (as meteorites), they may even be useful to us on Earth. About $^1/_{10}$ of the asteroids that strike Earth are almost pure nickel-iron. Thousands of years ago, before humans learned how to get iron from ores, meteorites were the only supply of iron. Iron was valuable for making tools. Even today, humans are mining metals made available by asteroids. The Sudbury Basin in Canada is known for its nickel and iron deposits. A look from space shows that those deposits lie in a crater left by an asteroid that smacked into our planet millions of years ago. The asteroid did not actually bring the nickel and iron deposits found, but it may have helped the deposits form.

Above: Looking for iron, a prehistoric man examines a meteorite.

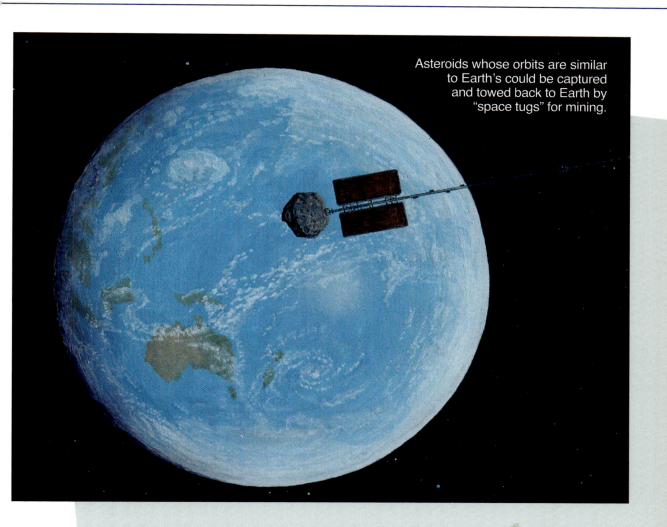

Asteroids whose orbits are similar to Earth's could be captured and towed back to Earth by "space tugs" for mining.

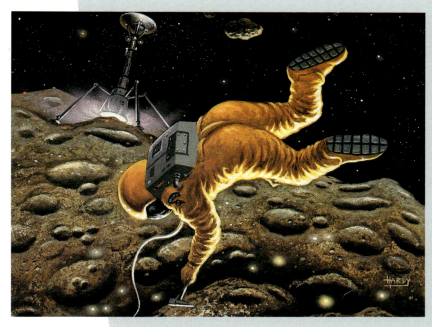

Left: An astronaut mines an asteroid in space in future times.

Journey to the Asteroid Belt

One reason astronomers want to study asteroids is that information about the substances composing these bodies can provide hints about what the early days of our Solar System were like. Up to now, scientists have used observations from Earth and from space probes to study asteroids. The probe *NEAR-Shoemaker* has even landed on an asteroid.

Some day, perhaps after humans have established a base on Mars, may venture farther outward usi manned spacecrafts. With Mars a base, astronauts might be able visit the asteroid belt for a close-analysis of some of its asteroids. Also, Ceres is quite far from the Sun, and this big asteroid would a very useful world on which to up telescopes and other instrume to study stars and distant planets

Above: A picture of NASA's *NEAR-Shoemaker* spacecraft.

A view of an Earthlike Mars from a base on one of Mars's moons. Future technology might make it possible to terraform Mars (make it like Earth). New gases could be put into Mars's atmosphere, thereby trapping sunlight and making the atmosphere like Earth's. Will Mars then become our springboard to the asteroids and beyond?

Right: An assortment of machinery at work in an asteroid-gathering mission. This artist's conception is based on an actual NASA study of the technology that would be needed to put an asteroid into permanent orbit around Earth.

Below: In this artwork, a team of asteroid explorers is greeted by a geyser. The matter shooting upward was once part of a comet that slammed into this otherwise desolate asteroid.

Future Resources

Asteroids might become humanity's new mines in centuries to come. There must be tens of thousands of asteroids that are made of iron. They could supply us with all the iron and steel we could ever want. In addition, some asteroids might serve as sources for other metals, as well as for oxygen, glass, concrete, and soil. Some are icy and might give us supplies of hydrogen, carbon, and nitrogen. These elements are not easy to obtain outside Earth, and they are necessary to humans in space. Some asteroids might even be hollowed out and made into space stations where people could live and work.

Above: In future times, could diamonds be mined from asteroids? It is quite possible, since some asteroids contain carbon, the material diamonds are made of. Here a team of miners examines its find as machines called mass drivers transport both mined materials and entire asteroids back to a base.

The asteroids — a jigsaw planet?

Why are some asteroids made mainly of iron, while others are made of rock or icy materials? If a planet like Earth broke up, pieces of its center would be iron, pieces of its surface would be icy, and pieces from in between would be rocky. Was there once a large planet between Mars and Jupiter that broke up? Maybe, but all the asteroids together would compose only a very small planet, and astronomers think it was too small to break up if it existed. Maybe there was not a planet there after all. Why, then, are there different kinds of asteroids? Scientists do not know.

A New Frontier

Asteroids will serve as starting points for more space exploration once people live on them. People from the asteroids could build rockets to take them to the moons of Jupiter, Saturn, and even farther. They might explore the entire Solar System. Perhaps some asteroids will be converted into huge starships, and thousands of people on them will drift outward, away from the Sun forever, on a long journey to the distant stars. Who knows? The asteroids might play an important role as human beings start to colonize the Galaxy and begin their quest for other forms of intelligent life.

Science fiction or science fact? A hollowed-out asteroid, now a fully equipped spaceship, cruises past Jupiter on a voyage out of the Solar System. Can you imagine people being born, growing up, raising families, and spending their entire lives as "space people" in ships like this? One day, it could happen.

An illustration, done to scale, of an assortment of asteroids — including most of the known asteroids with diameters of 125 miles (200 km) or more. All asteroids are sized in proportion to one another and to the edge of Mars on the left. The black-and-white illustration (*opposite, bottom*) is a guide to the names of each of the large asteroids, as well as to the Flora/Flores family of small asteroids.

Below: Some "firsts" and "bests" of the asteroids. Keep in mind that new asteroids are being discovered all the time and that records are made to be broken — even astronomical ones.

Record Set	Asteroid	Comments
Largest asteroid in asteroid belt	**Ceres**	Diameter: 590 miles (950 km)
Brightest asteroid	**Vesta**	Only member of asteroid belt visible to naked eye
Shortest known rotation (spinning) period	**1998 KY$_{26}$**	10.7 minutes
Longest known rotation	**Glauke**	1,200 hours
First asteroid to be discovered	**Ceres**	January 1, 1801
First asteroid to be discovered photographically	**Brucia**	December 20, 1891
Shortest time to revolve around Sun	**1999 KW$_4$**	188 days (orbit is within that of Earth)
Longest time to revolve around Sun	**2000 CR$_{105}$**	17,547.8 years (orbit is in the outer Solar System)
First asteroid moon to be photographed	**Ida**	Ida and its moon, Dactyl, were observed by the *Galileo* spacecraft in 1993.
First masculine name for an asteroid	**Eros**	1898
First spacecraft landing on an asteroid	**Eros**	*NEAR-Shoemaker* landed on Eros in 2001.

Fact File: The Asteroids

Thousands upon thousands of them exist, and they come in a variety of sizes and shapes. They look like bricks, dumbbells, mountains, cosmic sausages, potatoes, and even the island of Manhattan. They are named Iris, Flora, Davida, Cincinnati, Marilyn, Russia, and Claudia.

One is even called Photographica, in honor of photography — at one time a brand-new way to discover them in space.

We call them planetoids, minor planets, and, when they stray from their orbits, meteoroids. They are the asteroids.

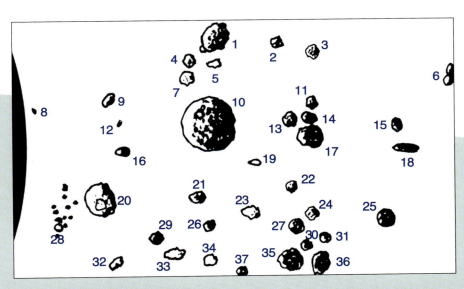

Key

1 Pallas	14 Themis	27 Europa
2 Winchester	15 Hermione	28 Flora/Flores
3 Euphrosyne	16 Fortuna	29 Egeria
4 Bamberga	17 Hygiea	30 Ursula
5 Daphne	18 Camilla	31 Alauda
6 Hector	19 Dembowska	32 Hebe
7 Juno	20 Vesta	33 Eunomia
8 Eros	21 Eugenia	34 Herculina
9 Iris	22 Diotima	35 Interamnia
10 Ceres	23 Psyche	36 Davida
11 Bettina	24 Lorely	37 Siegena
12 Nysa	25 Cybele	
13 Patientia	26 Thisbe	

More Books about Asteroids

Asteroid Impact. Douglas Henderson (Dial Books)

Asteroids, Comets, and Meteors. Robin Kerrod (Lerner)

Asteroids, Comets, and Meteors. Gregory Vogt (Raintree Steck-Vaughn)

Collision Course! Cosmic Impacts and Life on Earth. Alfred Bortz (Millbrook Press)

Comets and Asteroids. E. M. Hans (Raintree Steck-Vaughn)

Comets, Asteroids, and Meteorites. Roy A. Gallant (Benchmark Books)

DK Space Encyclopedia. Nigel Henbest and Heather Couper (DK Publishing)

CD-ROMs

Comet Explorer. (Cyanogen)

Exploring the Planets. (Cinegram)

Web Sites

The Internet is a good place to get more information about asteroids. The web sites listed here can help you learn about the most recent discoveries, as well as those made in the past.

KidsAstronomy. www.kidsastronomy.com/

Near-Earth Asteroid Tracking. neat.jpl.nasa.gov/

Near-Earth Asteroid Rendezvous Mission. near.jhuapl.edu/

Nine Planets. www.nineplanets.org/asteroids.html

Views of the Solar System. www.solarviews.com/eng/asteroid.htm

Places to Visit

Here are some museums and centers where you can find a variety of space exhibits.

Canada Science and Technology Museum
1867 St. Laurent Boulevard
100 Queen's Park
Ottawa, Ontario K1G5A3
Canada

Henry Crown Space Center
Museum of Science and Industry
57th Street and Lake Shore Drive
Chicago, IL 60637

NASA Glenn Research Center
Educational Services Office
21000 Brookpark Road
Cleveland, OH 44135

National Air and Space Museum
Smithsonian Institution
7th and Independence Avenue SW
Washington, DC 20560

Odyssium
11211 142nd Street
Edmonton, Alberta T5M 4A1
Canada

Sydney Observatory
Observatory Hill
Sydney, New South Wales 2000
Australia

Glossary

asteroid belt: the space between the orbits of Mars and Jupiter that contains most of the asteroids in the Solar System.

asteroids: very small "planets." Hundreds of thousands of them exist in our Solar System. Most of them orbit the Sun between Mars and Jupiter.

Centaurs: small bodies between the orbits of Jupiter and Neptune. The Centaurs in ancient Greek myths were half horse and half human.

Ceres: the first asteroid to be discovered. It has a diameter of 590 miles (950 km) and is the biggest asteroid in the asteroid belt.

Eros: the first asteroid to receive a masculine name. In 2001, the probe *NEAR-Shoemaker* landed on Eros. Eros is about 20 miles (32 km) long and has a diameter of about 4.5 miles (7 km).

galaxies: the numerous large groupings of stars, gas, and dust that exist in the Universe. Our Galaxy is known as the Milky Way.

Hector: an unusual asteroid that seems to be shaped like a dumbbell.

Kuiper belt: small bodies in the region of the Solar System lying beyond Neptune. They seem to mostly resemble icy comets, but some may be rocky asteroids.

meteor: a meteoroid that has entered Earth's atmosphere. Also, the bright streak of light made as the meteoroid enters or moves through the atmosphere.

meteorite: a meteoroid when it hits Earth.

meteoroid: a lump of rock or metal drifting through space. Meteoroids can be as large as small asteroids, or they can be as small as specks of dust.

minor planet: another name for an asteroid.

NASA: the space agency in the United States — the National Aeronautics and Space Administration.

near-Earth asteroid: an asteroid or comet whose orbit takes it near Earth's orbit.

planetoid: another name for an asteroid. In a way, this is a more accurate name, since the asteroids are more "planetlike" than they are "starlike."

Pluto: the farthest planet in our Solar System. It is so small that some astronomers believe it actually is a large asteroid.

Solar System: the Sun with the planets and all other bodies, such as asteroids, that orbit the Sun.

terraform: to make a planet or other large body in space suitable for human life.

trapped asteroids: asteroids that are captured by the gravity of planets.

Trojans: two groups of asteroids that travel in the same orbit around the Sun as Jupiter. One group goes before the planet, and the other follows behind.

Universe: everything that we know exists and that we believe may exist.

Vesta: the brightest asteroid. It has a diameter of about 326 miles (525 km).

Index

Born in 1920, Isaac Asimov came to the United States as a young boy from his native Russia. As a young man, he was a student of biochemistry. In time, he became one of the most productive writers the world has ever known. His books cover a spectrum of topics, including science, history, language theory, fantasy, and science fiction. His brilliant imagination gained him the respect and admiration of adults and children alike. Sadly, Isaac Asimov died shortly after the publication of the first edition of *Isaac Asimov's Library of the Universe.*

The publishers wish to thank the following for permission to reproduce copyright material: front cover, 3, NASA/JPL; 4, Courtesy of Southwest Research Institute; 5, © David Hardy; 6, 7, © Lynette Cook 1988; 8, National Space Science Data Center; 9, National Space Science Data Center and the Team Leader, Dr. Michael J. S. Belton, The Galileo Project; 10, © Sally Bensusen 1988; 11, © Julian Baum 1988; 12 (upper), © David Hardy; 12 (lower), Melissa Valuch/© Gareth Stevens, Inc. 2002; 13, NASA/JPL; 14, National Space Science Data Center; 15, © Julian Baum 1988; 16 (upper), © James M. Baker; 16 (lower), © David Milon; 17, 18, NASA; 19, NASA/JPL; 20, © David Hardy 1987; 21 (upper), © William K. Hartmann; 21 (lower), © David Hardy 1987; 22, NASA; 23, © David Hardy; 24 (upper), NASA; 24 (lower), © Kurt Burmann 1988; 25, © Mark Maxwell 1988; 26-27, © David Hardy 1987; 28, © Andrew Chaikin.